Careers without College

Child Care Worker

by Kathryn A. Quinlan

Consultant:

Alice Burton
Research Coordinator
Center for the Child Care Workforce

CAPSTONE
HIGH/LOW BOOKS
an imprint of Capstone Press
Mankato, Minnesota

Capstone High/Low Books are published by Capstone Press
818 North Willow Street • Mankato, MN 56001
http://www.capstone-press.com

Library of Congress Cataloging-in-Publication Data
Quinlan, Kathryn A.
    Child care worker/by Kathryn A. Quinlan.
       p. cm. — (Careers without college)
    Includes bibliographical references and index.
    Summary: Outlines the job responsibilities of child care workers, the working
environment, training required, and job prospects.
    ISBN 0-7368-0032-8
    1. Child care—Vocational guidance—United States—Juvenile literature. 2. High
school graduates—Employment—United States—Juvenile literature. 3. Child care
workers—United States—Juvenile literature. [1. Child care—Vocational guidance.
2. Vocational guidance.] I. Title. II. Series: Careers without college (Mankato, Minn.)
HQ778.7.U6Q56 1999
362.71'2'02373—dc21
                                                98-7185
                                                CIP
                                                  AC

Editorial Credits
Kimberly J. Graber, editor; James Franklin, cover designer and illustrator;
    Sheri Gosewisch, photo researcher
Photo Credits
Barbara Stitzer, cover
Dave Luchansky, 30
Jim West, 12
Kevin Vandivier, 35
Leslie O'Shaughnessy, 4, 9, 11, 18, 24, 26, 28, 32, 44
PhotoBank Inc./Lafayette, 22; Spencer Grant, 38, 41
Photo Network/Myrleen Cate, 16
Shaffer Photography/James L. Shaffer, 36
Transparencies Inc./Tom and Dee Ann McCarthy, 14, 20
Visuals Unlimited/Mark E. Gibson, 6

Table of Contents

Fast Facts 5

Chapter 1   What Child Care Workers Do 7

Chapter 2   What the Job Is Like 19

Chapter 3   Training 27

Chapter 4   Salary and Job Outlook 33

Chapter 5   Where the Job Can Lead 37

Words to Know 42

To Learn More 45

Useful Addresses 46

Internet Sites 47

Index 48

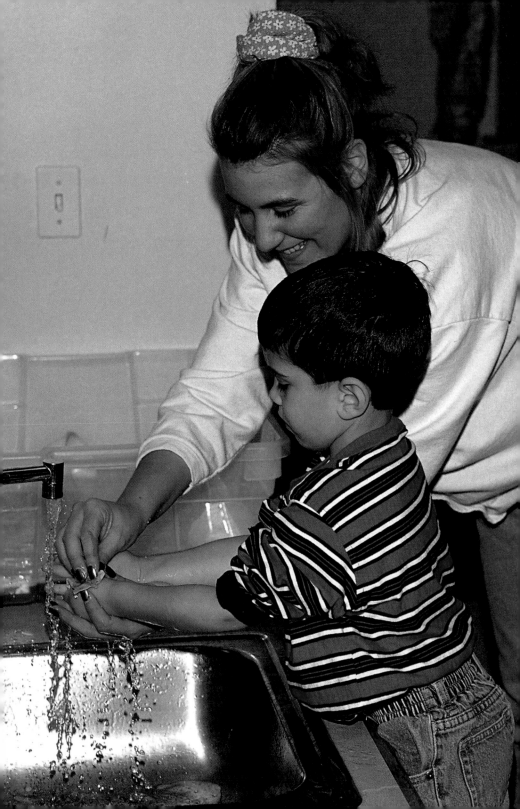

Fast Facts

Career Title_____Child care worker

Minimum Educational_____U.S.: high school diploma
Requirement   Canada: high school diploma

Certification Requirement_____U.S.: varies by state
                                Canada: varies by province

Salary Range_____U.S.: $7,280 to $20,280
(U.S. Bureau of Labor Statistics and   Canada: $7,300 to $46,700
Human Resources Development
Canada, late 1990s figures)   (Canadian dollars)

Job Outlook_____U.S.: faster than average growth
(U.S. Bureau of Labor Statistics and   Canada: stable
Human Resources Development
Canada, late 1990s projections)

DOT Cluster_____Service occupations
(Dictionary of Occupational Titles)

DOT Number_____359.677-018

GOE Number_____10.03.03
(Guide for Occupational Exploration)

NOC_____6473
(National Occupational Classification—Canada)

Chapter 1

What Child Care Workers Do

Child care workers care for children when parents cannot. Some child care workers take care of children every day while parents work. Others care for children whose parents must leave them for short periods of time.

Child care workers' duties vary depending on where they work. Most child care workers have basic care duties and teaching duties. They also

Most child care workers have teaching duties.

plan and perform administrative tasks such as keeping records and handling money.

Basic Care

Basic care duties include keeping children healthy, safe, and clean. Child care workers help children stay healthy in many ways. They feed healthful meals and snacks to children. They make sure children wear warm clothes in cold weather and light clothes in warm weather. Child care workers watch children for signs of illness and contact parents if children seem ill.

Child care workers try to keep children safe from accidents and injuries. They watch children carefully to help them avoid dangerous situations. Child care workers also use preventive measures. For example, they look for objects that might hurt children and move them out of reach.

Child care workers must know what to do if accidents happen. They care for children who

Child care workers make sure children wear warm clothes in cold weather.

get hurt. Child care workers clean and bandage small cuts. They contact parents if children are hurt and take badly hurt children to hospitals for care.

Many child care workers learn basic first aid to treat children who get hurt. They also may learn cardiopulmonary resuscitation (CPR). CPR is a method of saving people who stop breathing or whose hearts have stopped. It involves breathing into a victim's mouth. CPR also involves pressing on a victim's chest in a certain pattern.

Child care workers help children with basic hygiene. Child care workers make sure children wash their hands before eating and after using the bathroom. Child care workers also may bathe or diaper young children.

Teaching

Child care workers teach children important skills. They help children remember ideas they learn in school or from their parents. Child care workers plan games and activities that help children learn.

Child care workers use books to teach children. Children learn new words when they read books and hear stories. Children also learn about many

Child care workers use books to teach children.

Child care workers teach children social skills.

subjects from books. Stories sometimes help children understand other people's feelings.

Child care workers help children learn to communicate. They ask children questions about stories. They invite children to share show-and-tell objects. Children talk about their objects to other children during show-and-tell. These activities teach children to put their thoughts into words.

Many child care workers plan art projects for children. Workers help children paint, cut and paste paper, and color pictures. These activities teach children to work with their hands. Art projects also can teach children about subjects such as events, seasons, colors, and numbers.

Child care workers teach children social skills. They encourage children to play well together. They teach children to share and to take turns. Child care workers encourage children not to fight with one another. They also teach children to work together to accomplish tasks.

Child care workers help children gain self-esteem. Self-esteem is a feeling of pride and respect for oneself. Child care workers encourage children to try new tasks. Children feel proud when

they accomplish new tasks. Child care workers praise children for good behavior.

Planning and Administrative Tasks
Most child care workers plan each day they spend with children. Child care workers care for children of all ages. They must plan activities for babies, toddlers, and school children.

Child care workers must understand all stages of child development to plan activities. Two-year-old children behave differently than five-year-old children. Children gain skills and abilities as they grow. Child care workers plan activities based on the ages of the children in their care.

Child care workers also must understand that each child is different. Some children learn more quickly than other children. Some children read well. Other children sing or draw well.

Child care workers care for children of all ages.

Child care workers plan activities that help each child learn in his or her own way.

Child care workers plan children's time to help them stay fit. Children need to be active. Child care workers plan time for children to run and play. Children also need time to rest. Child care workers plan time for children to nap or play quietly.

Child care workers' administrative tasks differ from job to job. Many child care workers collect money from parents and pay bills. They keep records of each child's progress. Child care workers have more administrative duties if they run their own child care businesses. They must keep records of their earnings and pay taxes.

Child care workers help each child learn in his or her own way.

Chapter 2

What the Job Is Like

Child care is hard work. Most workers enter the child care field because they enjoy working with children. They take pride in helping children learn.

Child care can be tiring. Child care workers spend hours on their feet. They often bend down to take care of children. Child care workers must move quickly to keep up with young children.

Child care workers spend hours on their feet.

Some child care workers care for children in homes.

Most child care workers follow daily routines. They serve snacks or settle children down for naps at the same time each day. Children feel more secure when they follow routines. They learn more easily when they feel secure.

Work Settings

Many child care workers have jobs at child care centers. They may work for public or private child care centers. State governments fund and direct public child care centers. Individuals and community groups operate private child care centers.

People in the child care field work in many other settings. Some work at churches or schools. Some child care workers care for children in parents' homes. Others work in their own homes.

Child care workers may work together if they care for many children. Laws require one worker to care for a limited number of children. Day care centers must have enough workers to care for all the children.

Working Hours

Child care workers in child care centers often work long hours. Parents bring children to child care centers before they go to work. Some children

Children must be watched at all times.

arrive at child care centers at seven o'clock in the morning or earlier. Many parents cannot pick up their children until five o'clock in the evening or later.

Child care workers also work long hours if they work in homes. Children arrive at child care workers' homes early in the morning. Child care workers who work in parents' homes must arrive before parents leave for work. They stay until parents return from work.

Child care workers take few breaks. Children must be watched at all times. Workers can take turns having breaks if there are several workers.

Many child care workers at child care centers work part-time. Centers may hire people to work in shifts. Home child care workers find it difficult to work part-time. They must work as long as parents work. Many parents work full-time.

Personal Qualities

People who work with young children must be patient. Each day has new challenges for child care workers. They must be able to handle unexpected events. Children can be easily upset and difficult to manage if they are tired. A child who does not feel well may need extra attention.

Child care workers must be friendly but firm. They should be quick to praise children. Child

care workers also must be able to set rules. Children need to learn to follow rules and play well together.

Children learn from child care workers by watching them and listening to what they say. Child care workers must set good examples and use proper language. Child care workers should be polite, kind, and clean. They also should be able to explain ideas in simple ways.

Child care workers should be in good shape. They must keep up a fast pace for many hours at a time. Child care workers need to have a great deal of energy and enthusiasm.

Creative skills can help child care workers. Child care workers plan music, art, and storytelling activities for children. They also help children complete these activities.

Child care workers spend most of their time walking, standing, or bending.

Chapter 3

Training

Training requirements for U.S. child care workers vary by state. Each state decides how much training and education its public child care workers should have. Private child care centers may have fewer requirements. Most U.S. child care workers must have high school diplomas.

Canada also has varying training requirements for child care workers. Some employers require community college diplomas. Others may require special training or experience. Most child care workers in Canada have high school diplomas.

Each state decides how much training its public child care workers should have.

Child care centers also have their own training requirements for workers. Many employers hire workers only if they have taken child development classes at community colleges. These classes teach workers how children learn and grow. Most child care centers have on-the-job training programs. Other centers require workers to take additional classes after they start work. Many employers also require child care workers to take first aid and CPR courses.

Child Development Associates

Some states and employers prefer child care workers to be Child Development Associates (CDAs). CDAs have proven they are qualified to care for children. The Council for Early Childhood Professional Recognition awards the CDA title to individual child care workers.

People must meet certain requirements if they want to be CDAs. They must have 120 hours of child care training and a high school diploma. They also must have 480 hours of child care experience.

Child care centers have their own requirements for workers.

The Council for Early Childhood Professional Recognition offers a one-year training program. People can complete this program to gain the required training and experience.

Workers then must prove that they have the required knowledge and skills. They complete a series of exercises to demonstrate their skills. Council members also question workers about their knowledge of child care practices. Workers who pass these final reviews become CDAs.

What Students Can Do Now

Students interested in the child care field can gain experience in many ways. They can volunteer at child care centers, schools, or camps. Volunteers offer to do a job without pay. Students can lead clubs or coach athletic teams. They may find part-time jobs or summer jobs working with children.

Students can use volunteer work and part-time jobs to find out if they enjoy working with children. Students also can find out if they have the patience and energy needed to care for children.

Child Development Associates have proven they are qualified to care for children.

Chapter 4

Salary and Job Outlook

Child care workers with education and experience receive the highest earnings. They also are more likely to find opportunities for advancement. Today, many jobs are available in the child care field.

Salary

Child care workers earn different salaries in different work settings. Workers in family child

---

Child care workers earn different salaries in different work settings.

care homes usually earn less than workers in child care centers. Most child care workers in the United States earn between $7,280 and $20,280 per year (all figures late 1990s). The average salary for full-time child care workers in the United States is about $13,000 per year.

The average salary for child care workers in Canada is about $26,000 per year. The highest paid child care workers earn up to $46,700. The lowest paid child care workers earn about $7,300 per year.

Job Outlook

Child care is a growing field in the United States and Canada for several reasons. Both parents have jobs in a growing number of households. These parents need good child care workers because they cannot be with their children.

Some companies help workers pay for child care. Companies offer to pay for child care as a

A growing number of companies operate day care centers for their workers' children.

benefit. Families can often afford child care if companies help them pay for it.

A growing number of companies operate day care centers for their workers' children. Companies put these centers in their buildings. The centers offer employment opportunities for child care workers.

Chapter 5

Where the Job Can Lead

Child care workers have a few ways to advance. Some child care workers advance by gaining experience and training. They may earn higher pay. They may advance to manage other child care workers.

Other Child Care Opportunities
Some child care workers open their own child care businesses. People who operate child care

Some child care workers open their own child care businesses.

centers must have some business skills. They also must follow state laws regarding child care businesses.

Some child care workers take jobs in fields related to child care. They may become advocates for child care issues. Child care advocates work to ensure that child care is safe, of good quality, and available to everyone. Other child care workers may work for companies that help people find child care.

Related Fields

Some child care workers advance to different careers related to children. Most of these careers require additional education. Some require licenses. A license gives people official permission to perform a certain job.

Some child care workers become teachers. Public school teachers must have four-year degrees. A degree is a title given by a college or university. Public school teachers also must have

Some child care workers become teachers.

licenses. Teachers have licenses to teach particular grade levels or subjects. For example, a teacher may have a license to teach high school science. Private school teachers may not be required to have degrees or licenses.

Child care workers may become child psychologists or psychiatrists. They may help children with behavior problems or learning problems. Child psychologists and psychiatrists have advanced college degrees and licenses.

Child psychologists often work in schools. Child psychiatrists are medical doctors and can prescribe medicines. They often work in offices and clinics. People with backgrounds in child care often do well in these fields.

Teachers have licenses to teach particular grade levels or subjects.

Words to Know

benefit (BEN-uh-fit)—a payment or service in addition to a salary or wages

cardiopulmonary resuscitation (kar-dee-oh-PUHL-muh-nair-ee ri-suhss-uh-TAY-shuhn)---a method of saving people whose hearts have stopped; it involves breathing into victims' mouths and pressing on their chests in a certain pattern; also called CPR.

degree (di-GREE)—a title given by a college or university

development (di-VEL-uhp-muhnt)—the process of growing and learning

hygiene (HYE-jeen)—all the things people do to stay clean

license (LYE-suhnss)—official permission to do something

routine (roo-TEEN)—a set way of doing activities

self-esteem (SELF ess-TEEM)—a feeling of pride and respect for oneself

shift (SHIFT)—a set period of several hours of work

volunteer (vol-uhn-TEER)—to offer to do a job without pay

To Learn More

Cosgrove, Holli, ed. *Career Discovery Encyclopedia,* vol. 5. Chicago: J. G. Ferguson Publishing, 1997.

Eberts, Marjorie, and Margaret Gisler. *Careers in Child Care.* VGM Professional Careers. Lincolnwood, Ill.: VGM Career Horizons, 1994.

Paradis, Adrian A. *Careers for Caring People and Other Sensitive Types.* VGM Careers for You. Lincolnwood, Ill.: VGM Career Horizons, 1996.

Wittenberg, Renee. *Opportunities in Child Care Careers.* VGM Opportunities. Lincolnwood, Ill.: VGM Career Horizons, 1995.

Useful Addresses

Canadian Child Care Federation
30 Rosemount Avenue
Ottawa, Ontario K1Y 1P4
Canada

Center for the Child Care Workforce
733 15th Street NW
Suite 1037
Washington, DC 20005-2112

**Council for Early Childhood
  Professional Recognition**
2460 16th Street NW
Washington, DC 20009-3575

Internet Sites

The ABCs of Safe and Healthy Child Care
http://www.cdc.gov/ncidod/hip/abc/abc.htm

Canada Job Futures
http://www.hrdc-drhc.gc.ca/JobFutures/english/
volume1/647/647.htm

Caring for a Living
http://www.cfc-efc.ca/docs/00000281.htm

National Network for Child Care
http://www.nncc.org

**Occupational Outlook Handbook—Preschool
Teachers and Child Care Workers**
http://stats.bls.gov/oco/ocos170.htm

Index

activities, 10, 13, 15, 17, 25
advancement, 33
advocates, 39

benefit, 35

cardiopulmonary
    resuscitation, 10
Council for Early Childhood
    Professional Recognition,
    29, 31

development, 15, 29
duties, 7, 8, 17

earnings, 17, 33
education, 27, 33, 39
experience, 27, 29, 31, 33, 37

first aid, 10, 29

hygiene, 10
license, 39-40

psychiatrists, 40
psychologists, 40

routines, 20

salary, 33-34
self-esteem, 13
skills, 10, 13, 15, 25, 31, 39

teachers, 39-40
training, 27, 29, 31, 37

volunteers, 31